Prologue

Who sits before these pages, is o
I say to you, read on my friend, r

For I am reaching out to you, from every verse I speak
You are the one I look for, you are the one I seek

My secret thoughts are set before you now for all to see
The door is open to my world of truth and fantasy

Carl Roberts

Contents

Contents

Thoughts Of Childhood Days

On Christmas Day I couldn't wait
Like many other boys
And frantically I'd tear the wrappers
Off my brand new toys

That little boy of yesterday
Would think of Santa Claus
Whilst hanging up his stocking
What a special time it was

I thought a bird with long legs
And a beak down to the floor
Would visit certain houses
To leave babies at the door

Where did the moon go every night?
Who made the wind and rain?
Since I've known all the answers
Life has never been the same

That little boy of yesterday
Who thought of Santa Claus
Still thinks about his childhood days
What a special time it was

A Man and Boy In Wales *By Carl Roberts*

Freddie And Me

'Though Freddie used to play foot-ball
He wasn't very big at all
Considering that he was all
Of twenty one years old

To-gether we would kick that ball
Down there behind the school-yard wall
Sometimes we'd win, sometimes we'd fall
Or so I've heard it told

I reminisce and I recall
The blond haired Fred as he would sprawl
To overthrow and overhaul
And score the vital goal

I don't suppose we would enthral
The meagre crowd who would cat - call
Poor Fred because he was so small
And yet he was so bold

We'd play in sunshine, hail or squall
Down there behind the school - yard wall
Where blond haired Fred would give his all
Or so I've heard it told

Oh Mamma Can I Have My Favourite Breakfast?

Oh Mamma can I have my favourite breakfast?
You bought some yesterday at the shop
I've tried all the rest, but these are the best
Because they go snap, crackle and pop!
I love to watch them floating on the surface
So fresh and crispy, lovely and small
So Mamma can I have my favourite breakfast?
I want to snap and crackle them all!

Oh Mamma can I have my favourite breakfast?
Those little things Mr Kellog makes
I don't want All Bran. 'gone off' toast and jam
And I'm fed up with good old Corn Flakes
Ain't going to waste a teeny - weeny morsel
So when they're ready give me a call
Come on Mamma give me some breakfast
I've got to snap and crackle them all!

Oh Mamma can l have my favourite breakfast?
Coco Pops and Frosties are out
I've tried a few licks of those soggy Weetabix
But Rice Crispies are the ones l dream about!
Don't feed me Quaker Oats or Fruit and Fibre
And Sugar Puffs drive me up the wall
So Mamma can I have my favourite breakfast?
l want to snap and crackle them all!

(A boyhood memory)

Down In The Dingle Where The Water Flows

My mind goes back to yesterday
The sun shines and the soft breeze blows
I see a young boy playing there
Down in the Dingle where the water flows

It only seems a dream away
My shirt sleeves about my elbows
I see that little boy at play
Down in the Dingle where the water flows

I close my eyes and feel the sun
I smell the grass and no one knows
What I would give again to run
Down in the Dingle where the water flows

My mind goes back to yesterday
The sun shines and the soft breeze blows
I see a young boy playing there
Down in the Dingle where the water flows

(A boyhood memory)

Memory Of Home

Sometimes I feel so sad
When I think of Mam and Dad
And how they'd love to have me come to call

For it's not so long ago
When they'd greet me at the door
Lovely memories I cherish and recall

The house, the little street
And those friends I used to meet
Was there ever such a place in all the land?

Where time cannot erase
My tender memories of a place
Where once a little boy became a man

The Young Schoolboy

When I'd hear that school bell ring
I'd learn to read and write, and sing...

What is that picture on the wall, Miss, can you tell me please?
That is a map of the world my boy, with many lands and seas

Can we see our country Miss, where are the Welsh people from?
We are part of the British Isles boy, this, is where we belong

Please Sir, how do I find what forty-two is divided by six?
Work it out for yourself boy, and learn your mathematics

I can easily take away Sir, and do my addition with ease
But I can't do long division Sir, so will you help me please?

Who are they with the long beards Miss, and big swords in their hands?
They were known as Vikings boy, they came from the northern lands

How did they sail those long ships Miss, all the way to where we are?
They were very good sailors boy who were guided by the stars

Here's the story you asked me to write, will you mark it Sir for me?
It's a very interesting tale boy, but dot your I's and cross your t's

I've done every bit of my home work Sir, am I ready for my exam?
You must do better this year boy, just work as hard as you can

When I'd hear that school bell ring
I'd learn to read and write, and sing...

A Memory

Sometimes my mind goes back in time to when I was a kid
Where I can see a boy re-living all the things he did

From the time I was a youngster, a stripling in short trousers
When I'd play marbles down the lanes that ran between the houses

I was a lad, we never had a fridge or a TV
Before the days we double-glazed or heard of VAT

That happy home, that little nest, the Roberts family
Where Mam and Dad would do their best for sister and for me

Sister Sonia played piano, so much music in her fingers
We'd sing and dance together, oh, how the memory lingers

The school around the corner, it was just a street away
Where I was brought, and I was taught, I still recall the day

Where yesterday young girls would play, they'd skip and sing along
What simple pleasures filled their day, so happy was their song

With other boys I'd make a noise, a football at my feet
And read about Dan Dare while girls played hop-scotch in the street

And Christmas was so magical, what a special time it was
We'd open all the presents we'd received from Santa Claus

Sometimes my mind goes back in time to when I was a kid
Where I can see a boy re-living all the things he did

Mathematics

Mathematics, 'could never understand Mathematics
I wish they tried to teach me Acrobatics.
Well I could multiply and take-away with such precision
But when it came to taking on that long-division!

Mathematics, here's the story of my Mathematics
Why couldn't I have studied Amateur Dramatics?
But you know when looking back it seems such a shame
Was it in the teaching, or was I the one to blame?

History and Geography - couldn't wait to begin it
And when it came to English I just loved every minute!
Writing out an essay simply tilled me with elation
I'd dot my I's and cross my T's - no need for punctuation
I knew where each apostrophe and hyphen went in
I even studied words of Greek and Latin Origin!

But Mathematics, 'worse boy in the class at Mathematics
I'm sure I would have shone in Sub Aquatics!
I adored the myths and legends all about ancient Greece
But taking on Arithmetic was like Japanese!
Archimedes and Pythagoras were very clever men
But their theories and their principles just would not sink in!

Mathematics, a little more about Mathematics
I might as well have studied Aerobatics!
Those Algebraic formulas tied me in a knot
And Geometric calculations put me right on the spot!
I tried to do my very best each time don't you know
But I never knew where Decimal Points had to go!

Mathematics, just couldn't get a hold on Mathematics
Each time it left me cold, never once ecstatic
Now I knew about the Danube and its flow down to the sea
The Ganges and the Andes and the Isle of Capri
I loved Woodwork, Science Art and Music, even P.T.
But Mathematics!

Ode To Sam

He's just a dog I hear them say
A thing that'll bark and bite
Who sleeps around the house all day
When he's not in a fight
But have these voices known a friend
As faithful as old Sam?
Have they known the loyalty
A dog has for a man?

Here comes that scruffy dog again
I hear those voices say
As playful Sam runs down the lane
Out for a walk one day
But do these voices know
What it like to have a friend
Who's faithful to his master
Till his time is at an end

Sometimes his coat is dirty
When it's raining he's a mess
He's overweight, he's greedy
And his manners aren't the best
But tell me, what care I for those
Who scorn the friend of man
I have a friend, until the end
Who's name is simply .... Sam

Dedicated to Sam – My Cocker Spaniel 1974-1986 ... A Fine Dog

Remember The Year

Remember back in 'sixty one, you had a different kind of fun
When Elvis lived at number one and smoke got in your eyes.
And then along came 'sixty two you liked this girl and she liked you
But all you got was Asian flu much to your surprise !

Do you remember, how far did you get?
Do you remember, yes you do I bet
Do you remember, is it crystal clear?
Do you remember, remember the year.

Forgive me if I'm being bold, but it's no secret I've been told
You've been in love with rock'n'roll for thirty years or more
You'd play upon that old guitar, and dream someday you'd be a star
Before you even owned a car, in nineteen sixty four

Do you remember, how far did you get?
Do you remember, yes you do I bet
Do you remember, is it crystal clear?
Do you remember, remember the year

In February 'ninety three, you just turned half a century
The ravages of time I see are showing here and there
Along the way you've had your fun, sometimes you've lost sometimes
you've won
And I know you're not ready son to face that rockin' chair

Do you remember, how far did you get?
Yes you remember, yes you do I bet
Do you remember, is it crystal clear?
Do you remember, remember the year

Be Not Afraid (A Winter's Tale To Valerie)

Be not afraid of cold that winter time will bring
Amid the sounds of winter the happy Robin sings
He sings his songs of winter, our cheeky proud red-breast
While icy streams are shining by frosty fields caressed

Be not afraid of dark when winter nights soon fall
And as the cold air chills, you wrap around your shawl
The days fly by so quickly, the long nights passing slow
Be not afraid of darkness, the day-light soon will grow

Be not afraid of winter for springtime now is nigh
Adorn yourself with colours, soon comes your time to fly
The sunshine of the warmer days shall raise you from your gloom
And like a flower in sun-light, I shall watch you bloom

Eddie, Chuck And Buddy

Once upon a memory, when all the world was young
When Eddie, Chuck and Buddy saw their names at number one

I'd play upon my first guitar with fingers that were keen
And soon I found my way around that old music machine

And there was no denying that this thing was in my blood
For I grew up with Rock 'n' Roll, when music was so good

My radio supplied me with those hits of yesterday
Like 'Move it' and 'Apache', 'Peggy Sue' and 'Runaway'

Guitars, drums and harmonies, what special sounds they made
Before computers, discotheques and electronic aids

Well some would call this progress other folk would disagree
And somewhere in the middle, well, you'd probably find me

Someone who remembers the good friends he once found
Like Eddie, Chuck and Buddy, they were good to have around

So as I play this old guitar I wonder what went wrong
I long to hear the music, but where has the music gone?

The Robin

I sense a glimpse of red
And from my window see him there again
He's risen from his bed
Undaunted by the morning wind and rain

And when the frost has come
And light of shorter days flees to the west
While yearning for the sun
Our hopes are kept alive by his red-breast

So help him when you can
For what he seeks he cannot always find
When Winter is at hand
It threatens the survival of his kind

So when you see him there
Courageously defending what he can
Please show him that you care
And let the little Robin take his stand

A Man and Boy In Wales *By Carl Roberts*

Mother

I'm thinking of some one today
Who's always there when skies are grey
'Though other friends may come and go
Mothers's there for you, I know

For Mother is a some one
Who's so nice to have around
A shoulder you can lean upon
Who'll never let you down

She'll listen to your troubles
When no one seems to care
When everyone deserts you
Your Mother's always there

You may be so heart broken
Feeling like you'll never mend
But Mother's there to pick you up
Just like a special friend

And through the years her guidance
With loving words so true
Will shape your life
And make a better person out of you

'Though you may have your differences
It's you she's thinking of
When all is said and done
There's nothing like a Mother's love

I'm thinking of some one today
Who's always there when skies are grey...

Talk About America

Your shores I've yet to walk upon, and time is drifting by
I know not if my time will ever come
So many miles away across the ocean and the sky
As I look west into the setting sun

To far off Pennsylvania my Grandpa sailed away
To work the mines so many years ago
He came back home and told us all about the U.S.A.
He stayed awhile, then he was gone once more

He talked about America, I tried to understand
The story of this miner who met up with Uncle Sam
And now I know that if I ever reach the U.S.A.
They'll guarantee a boy like me will have a real nice day

I've heard a lot about you, all about the things you've seen
A civil war, a presidential race
I wonder where you're going, for I know just where you've been
I've seen those dusty footprints out in space

So talk about America, I'll try to understand
For Grandpa was a miner who met up with Uncle Sam
And now I know that if I ever reach the U.S.A.
You'll guarantee a guy like me will have a real nice day

Tell Me Something

Tell me something different
Tell me something new
Something that can lift my heart
The way you always do

Something nice to listen to
This dark and dreary day
Tell me something warm
To send this winter-time away

Tell me something cheerful
That lifts me for a while
When I'm feeling low I need
The glow that's in your smile

Tell me that I've won a prize
Or that my boat's come in
Or tell me there's no need
For me to go to work again!

Tell me that we're going off
To some where in the sun
Tell me it's Sorrento
Tell me ... life's begun!

(Thinking about Val whilst at York)

Despair Of Early Morn'

The day begins so cold and grey
The sky is dull and drawn
Of sun there is no sign, and all that I can find
Are fragments of my mind between each yawn

The flames are leaping in the hearth
And upward curls the smoke
And at this early hour, as hungry flames devour
I feel that I should cower 'neath their yoke

A glance outside up at the clouds
Shows me an angry sky
The rain comes into sight, soon day resembles night
And in the fading light I heave a sigh

I put away my walking shoes
Hang up the mongrel's chain
The walk will have to wait, until some later date
Meanwhile I curse my fate amid the rain

A Man and Boy In Wales *By Carl Roberts*

The Look That Says It All

I walk into the smoke filled room
And start to look around
The same old feeling's in the air
I recognise the sound
Some look up at the notices
Some lean against the wall
On everybody's face I see
The look that says it all

And everyone I see there
And every voice I hear
Is hoping, ever hoping
For something to appear
For they've known better times than these
They've never had to crawl
On everybody's face I see
The look that says it all

The room is almost full now
With people young and old
All searching for the same thing
As hard to find as gold
Without a job they're nothing
They've never felt so small
On everybody's face I see
The look that says it all

(A memory of a visit to the Job Centre)

What They Say About Love

Love comes to all kinds of people
There's nothing quite like it I know
It harbours so many descriptions
A few I have listed below

Love, said the man who had nothing, had given him reason to live
For in spite of his lowly position
He knew he had something to give

Love, said the man of possessions, was a treasure that often he'd sought
He'd silver and gold for the asking
But some things just cannot be bought

Love, said the amorous poet, inspires the word of my rhyme
Without it my verses are empty
To use it can make them sublime

Love, say articulate scholars,when composing their thoughts on a kiss
Is a passion unlike any other
'Tis a verb of exceptional bliss

Love, said the rock 'n' roll singer, is in every song that I choose
It's there when I'm singing a ballad
It's there when I'm singing the blues

Love, said the high rolling gambler, is a voice that I hear at my side
Sometimes it tells me to "fold 'em"
Sometimes it says "let 'em ride"

Love, said the old fortune teller, is waiting for you to command
Just look as you open your fingers
It's there in the palm of your hand

Love comes to all kinds of people
There's nothing quite like it I know...

Get Away

I've been to Greece and Turkey
And I've seen Mallorca too
'Seen lots of rain in sunny Spain
And one day in Corfu...
I sailed to Cassiopi
On a boat trip for the day
Well after all, you've got to get away

'Walked 'round the Colosseum
But the lions weren't at home
So then I bought a pizza
Well you know ... when in Rome
Tried the ice-cream in Sorrento
Or gelati as they say
Well after all, you've got to get away

I sampled the Canaries
Lanzarote was for me
The black sand and volcanoes
San Miguel was duty-free
I quite fancy a Paella
So I might go back one day
Well after all, you've got to get away

I'm looking at the rain
Which has forgotten how to stop
It's time I found myself a deal
Down at the travel shop
Then it's Calamine and After-Sun
And more mosquito spray
Well after all, you've got to get away!

Friend

I give my hand to everyman
As through this life I pass
You're welcome at my table
Break bread and fill your glass
To give is to receive, therefore
This message do I send
To everyman who takes my hand
Consider me your friend

Inspiration

Do you know my friend the poet?
Have you heard him tell his tales?
They are stories of his life
As a man and boy in Wales

We have a lot in common
Foe we know each other well
So it's really not surprising
'Though it can be strange to tell

For I've known all his acquaintances
The enemies and friends
Long before each verse was written
And the ink ran from his pen

For I'm the one he searches for
Each time he hears the call
Together we are strong
Should you divide us, we would fall

The poet needs my friendship
Like a beggar needs his bread
For he is lost without
My inspiration in his head

To Valerie My Love

I see the look on your sweet face
My thoughts recapturing
The way that happy smile's embrace
Has caused my heart to sing

A smile that puts the sun to shame
And made my senses race
So caused my heart to be aflame
As I beheld your face

'Twas then, as now, by stars above
I knew forever more
That you would always be my love
'Till seas desert the shore

Another Day

The six o'clock alarm bell rings
It's early morning once again
And weary eyes that long to sleep
Are waking from a slumber deep

I lay there drowsy from the call
Then sitting up I face the wall
I'm trying hard to be awake
Within my semi conscious state

A voice calls out inside my head
That says "wake up, get out of bed"
Reluctantly I find a way
To rise and face another day

I yawn across the bedroom floor
And stumble through the bathroom door
Sub-conciously I lunge and grope
Towards the shower and the soap

The water hits my lifeless skin
And stirs a weary soul within
Revitalised from head to toe
I have become a man once more!

And as my mind begins to see
The world unfold ahead of me
I smile, and to myself I say
"I'm ready for another day"

My Someone Else

When sitting all alone
Or laying peaceful in my bed
When all the world is silent
Something stirs within my head

I listen very carefully
And all at once I find
There is another one ....
Another me inside my mind

From deep inside I'm watching
I'm always there it seems
I'm someone else who listens
To my hopes and to my dreams

When in a situation
And decide which way to go
My someone deep inside
Is calling out and saying no

He'll tell me what he thinks
He'll say what he believes is true
Do I listen to myself or him?
I don't know what to do!

When you are sitting all alone
Or laying in your bed
When all the world is still
Does something stir inside your head?

Closing Down

He came out of the shower
And slammed his locker door
They wouldn't see old Charlie
In the lamp room anymore
And fifty-three just like him
Didn't like the news a bit
The notice on the wall said
They're closing down the pit

His heavy boots redundant
His torn cap needed mending
This didn't really matter now
His final shift was ending
He touched the blue scar on his head
Where once the flesh had split
And read the notice on the wall
They're closing down the pit

He read the names in silence
He'd known each one from birth
Side by side they'd toiled
Inside the bowels of the earth
He felt the valley dying
His anger made him spit
Old Charlie's on the scrap heap now
They're closing down the pit

The Scarlet Flower

We stand in silent memory
Of those who are no more
Remembering with pride
Our fallen comrades of the war

These unforgotten heroes of the past
Are not denied
Upon the nation's monuments
Their names are carved with pride

Remember then the gift of
Human sacrifice they gave
When you wear that scarlet flower
Lest we forget the brave

A Man and Boy In Wales *By Carl Roberts*

To Those Who Give Their Best

To those who give their best
Who sing their song when the heat is on
They don't cut corners, or mess around
And they always feel so duty bound

You'll find them pitching right in
Taking smooth with the rough when the going gets tough
They mean business., they can stand the test
Whatever they do, they do their best

They never think of giving up
When you need a hand, they'll understand
They'll jump from the fat to the frying pan
They' re going to help you if they can

So when that water gets too deep
And you think you might sink out of sight
Don't give in, don't run away
Do your best ... do it today

Aye Boy

Is that where you worked
In the dust and the noise?
Aye boy, that's the pit
Where I worked with the boys

Will you go back Dad
Across the incline?
No boy, no more
Now they've closed down the mine

Is anyone there Dad
To dig coal today?
No boy, we've all gone
They've swept us away

Is that where you worked
Where you dug out the coal?
Aye boy, that's the place
Where I was before the dole

Alcoholic

He tried to kick it many times
But every time he'd seem to lose
It wouldn't be an easy thing
To live his life without the booze

She came along, she tried to help
Stayed by him almost every night
Endeavouring to regulate
His alcoholic appetite

But could a way of life be changed
That was afflicted by desire
To fill another empty glass
With which to quench a hungry fire

She'd little hope against such odds
Of penetrating through his wall
When from within he answered to
The constant cry for alcohol

Child Sounds

The sound of children playing
Falls gentle on my ear
Their bright eyes and their laughter
The sweetest things to me

Within this happy picture
A smile looks out to me
A face I love so dearly
My child, my daughter dear

To hear the children singing
A sound we can't deny
To hear their infant voices
A tear comes to my eye

Just listen to their music
Could ever they be wrong
Their world is full of innocence
And happy is their song

A Man and Boy In Wales *By Carl Roberts*

The Miner

Have you seen his weary face
When he's dusty, cold and damp
As he ends another shift
With his "Tommy box" and lamp?

Have you seen them going down
In a cage like herded lambs
To their hovel far below
With the ponies and the trams?

Have you seen him walking there
As life turns his blackened pages
With his docket in his hand
As he goes to draw his wages?

Listen to his hungry cry
As his story he'll unfold
Of the day he lost his job
And his future, and his coal

Have you heard his mellow voice
When the choir sings along
When his music fills the valley
Have you heard the miner's song?

The Carpenter

He must be strong
He labours on, his challenges to meet
As work begins anew
He turns a willing screw
Whilst fallen shavings queue about his feet

He must not fail
And every nail that feels the hammer's force
Is destined on that day
A greater part to play
His steady hand will not delay the course

The sawdust flies
And 'though his eyes are weary from the dust
You'll not hear him complain
He'll work against the grain
The Carpenter remains to earn his crust

Upon Our Very Streets

"They broke into my place"
Like many more I'd heard before
This bitter cry was angered by
A modern scourge upon the human race

"They stole the bag and fled,
and worse, the contents of my purse
were all I had, I feel so mad,
Why me, why not somebody else?," she said

With no respect for women,
And even less for men
This modem epidemic has been freed
To terrorise the innocent
What answer is there when
Upon our very streets this vermin breed

"They took my car again,
you're right, that's twice, oh what a price
society demands of me
does anybody hear when I complain?"

With no respect for women
And even less for men
No matter how we argue and we plead
They terrorise the innocent
What answer is there when
Upon our very streets this vermin breed

My Friend

In the evening time amid the fast and fading light
I walk among the shadows just before the coming night
To you my thoughts are reaching as this day draws to an end
How empty life would be without my friend

You've always stood beside me even when sometimes we've found
The road to happiness has led us over stony ground
So now I'll not concern myself when life becomes unfair
For I'll get by, as long as you are there

So as the evening passes and another night I see
It gives me strength to know that where I am is where you'll be
You are the rock I lean upon, and so I say again
How empty life would be without my friend

A Man and Boy In Wales *By Carl Roberts*

Vocabulary

To use a word like pedigree
Could well describe the breeding
And if a chap is famished
Chances are he could need feeding
It's all to do with choosing the right word you see
And learning our vocabulary

When I'm saturated
Well, I couldn't get much wetter
Old Charlies's convalescing
So I think he's getting better
We'll find a way to say it, just wait and see
By learning our vocabulary

When you are incognito
You will be in a disguise
See an optometrist
And he'll look you in the eyes
Oh, soon we'll have a memory like a dictionary
When learning our vocabulary

When people are fastidious
They're fussy, hard to please
Unlike the undemanding type
With whom you feel at ease
But who knows, some or those may like my poetry
And even my vocabulary!

A Lesson Learned From Man's Mistake

Of all the creatures born to die
I contemplate and wonder why
When on the ground I see him crawl
Why he's allowed to live at all

Inhabiting the land and sea
In many lands his kind will be
He's found in varied length and size
This creature that I so despise

Without the aid of claws or hooves
This wretched form below me moves
Forbidding eyes lay waiting there
And gaze with their hypnotic stare

Stalking his prey by smell and sight
He poisons with his deadly bite
And writhing contours of his mould
Possess the power to crush you cold

From days of Adam and of Eve
A serpent lived I do believe
And from a tree he did invite
The man below to take a bite

And from that day so long ago
When Satan tempted Adam so
A lesson learned from his mistake
Must be ... to never trust a snake

Size Of The Guys

Just open your eyes
And look at the size
Of some of the guys at the bar

There's many that could be
The size that they should be
Instead of the sizes they are

With bellies that bulge
From the way the indulge
You'd think they'd be better by far

Being fussy and choosy
No wonder the booziness
Makes them the way that they are

They don't hear our sighs
As we look to the skies
For they have their eyes on a jar

So open your eyes
When you look at the size
Of some of the guys at the bar

She's A Woman

Oh she used to run to me
With those ribbons in her hair
And I'd sit her on my knee
Now I sit and wonder where
Where those yesterdays have gone
All those lovely used-to-be's
Oh, why couldn't they go on?
I can't believe that she's a woman

So I had to say goodbye
To the ribbons and the bows
To the wonder in her eyes
And those freckles on her nose
To her standing at the door
Sometimes laughter, sometimes tears
Did it really have to go?
I can't believe that she's a woman

So I put my thoughts away
For they're from another world
Where a Mam and Dad would play
With a blue-eyed little girl
Now I see her at my door
And I'm smiling through my tears
She's no baby anymore
I can't believe that she's a woman

A Man and Boy In Wales *By Carl Roberts*

Brain

'Would be an insult to a friend
Therefore my brain I can't offend
By feeding him commercials from TV
I promised Brain sometime ago
He'd never have to stoop that low
I'd better things lined up for him and me

Before the waiting TV set's
A place I hardly ever get
When day is done and evening falls again
For there's a place I'd rather be
And pray that Brain will rescue me
As I reach out for paper and a pen

The garbage that is beamed our way
Brain-washing millions everyday
With murder, sex and violent fantasy
Continues to contaminate
The countless viewers as they wait
But I won't let it get to Brain and me

So to the mass that cannot cope
Unless they watch their daily soap
From Aus' to Emmerdale or the East End
Switch off before you go insane
Come on now, don't insult your brain
That bloomin "box" will drive you 'round the bend!

Millie

Millie is a Spaniel
The white and orange kind
Just like the one that's pictured
On that birthday card of mine

I think she has the droopiest
And saddest eyes in town
But I know there's a happy dog
Beneath that furrowed frown

It's just the way that Spaniel's look
Beleaguered, down at heel
Well, how are they supposed to say
Exactly how they feel

She'll wag her little tail a bit
To signal all is well
Now if she was a budgie
I suppose she'd ring her bell!

Some days when she is '"out of sorts"
Her tail between her legs
She'll mope around the house all day
Her eyes like two poached eggs!

Then all at once she's bouncing back
A miracle, behold,
Those eyes have found their sparkle
And that little nose is cold

She'll bring a slipper or a ball
To greet me at the door
And then we'll have a cuddle...
That's what Spaniels are for

(In memory of a wonderful pet)

A Man and Boy In Wales *By Carl Roberts*

There Goes Another One

There goes another one
Tell me, what does he do it for?
And here comes another one
Don't they know they're breakin' the law?

What can we do with them?
They're buzzing all around us like a curse
How should we deal with them?
The current situation's getting worse

He gives no indication
To show he's turning here
So he's forcing me to slow-down
Back into second gear!

And look, she's doing sixty
Driving in a slow-down zone
Busy talking to her boy-friend
On her shiny mobile phone

There goes another one
Flying down the avenue
Chased by another one
Going so fast - radio blasting too!

What can we do with them?
They pay no heed to miles-per-hour signs
How should we deal with them?
Parking on those double amber lines

Now he pulls out of a "lay-by"
Forcing me to "hit the brake"
And there's someone's in my mirror
Who can't wait to over-take!

As I approach a roundabout
He jumps into my lane
And then he "jams the brakes on"
Blimey, is this guy insane?

What can we do with them?
Have they ever read the Highway Code?
How should we deal with them?
C'mon someone get 'em off the road!

How I Wish I Could Play The Piano
(a dream)

How I wish I could play the piano -
How I long to command every note
The black ones and the white ones too
Then some day I could play for you
A work from the pen of Mozart
I'd even impress my friends
With a Rondo or a Sonata
Timeless music that never ends

How I wish I could play the piano
All those melodies that we all know
I'd name a song and find the key
And just to show what I could be,
I'd perform compositions by Chopin
A composer so worthy of praise
With a Prelude or a Mazurka
Minute waltz or Polonaise

How I wish I could play the piano
Oh to know all those sharps and flats
With finger-tips that would seldom rest
I'd practice hard and soon progress
To a certain arrangement by Gershwin
It's called Rhapsody In Blue
Oh, I wish I could play the piano
Don't you wish that you could too!

That's What Matters To Me

To me it matters not
If you're cool or hot
Or if you possess
A little or a lot
For in the end
Each one of you is my friend
And that's what matters to me

And I don't care
If you're dark or fair
If you like the Beatles
Or what clothes you wear
It's just good to find
You're all friends of mine
And that's what matters to me

It's so good to see
You all feel like me
For we're all God's children
One big family
I give thanks today
You've all come my way
And that's what matters to me

On Her Way (One of Caron's school days)

The breeze blows gently through her hair
She skips along, without a care
And as she goes he's standing there
She's on her way, on her way to school

Her teeth are brushed, her shoes are clean
Her uniform is grey and green
And all the while he's not been seen
She's on her way, on her way to school

She'll learn to read and write today
She'll multiply, and take - away
Her Daddy's watched her and he'll say
She's on her way,on her way to school

Ancient Grease!

The girls walk by in their bikinis
Fat ones, tall ones, some just weenies
White skins, red skins, some dark brown
Bottoms covered, top halves gone!
In February they would freeze
But now it's June in sunny Greece

There's lager sold along the beach
To get to parts that some can't reach
There's Dutch and Swedes and German folks and ...
I've even heard some English spoken
'Haven't seen any faggots and peas
They don't cook these in ancient grease!

Here comes Spiro with the beers
Shouting out the Greek for cheers
Standing there upon the sand
A pile of euros in his hand
I think I'll have some Feta cheese
Do they make it in ancient grease?

The smell of lotions fill the air
We're splashing on Ambre Solaire
With sun block on the nose and lips
We sit and fry like greasy chips
Hoping that our tans increase
We're sizzling in ancient grease!!

Archie – Born March 1st, 2010

After many years of waiting
A grandson came along
To Caron and Miles, a lovely child
With golden hair and blue eyes was born

So Archie completes our family
Where we feel so content ... and then
This angel can change to a demon
Full of mischief and mayhem!

Before he could walk he was running
Falling about all the time
Nothing he faced seemed too hard for him
And he took it all on with a smile

He's such a happy little chap
Full of wickedness too don't you know
Sometimes we end up in a flap
Not knowing which way to go!

God knew we could cope with a rascal
Each day we give thanks (with a sigh)
He could have made him a little easier
But somehow, we know, we'll get by!

We know he'll grow up to be special
For he has many talents you see
But his greatest gift is his family
Who make him richer than many will be

A Man and Boy In Wales *By Carl Roberts*

We Must Have Played 'em All!

All aboard the Transit van
Foot down, a scream of tyres
With "Dickie Bows" and jackets
Drums, guitars and amplifiers

We've driven on the motorways
Crawled up those valley roads
There's not a club in South Wales
Where we haven't trod the boards

And they'd always keep a welcome
In a place we still recall
On a Friday night on Beddau
Down at the Welfare Hall

We'd do the Ponderosa
For old Charlie any night
Even go to Milford Haven
If the price was right!

Seven Sisters, Ystradgynlais
Or up to Maerdy Hall
To Crynant, Neath or Abercrave
We must have played 'em all

We've played up in the Rhondda
Where once they dug for coal
Had a curry in Ton Pentre
After singing rock 'n' roll

And on to Caesar's Palace
In good old Trecco Bay
Where Carl and Dai and Malcolm
Would rock the night away!

And what about the Hillside Club
Now there's a little gem
We'd have 'em on the dance floor
From twelve 'till two a.m

So here's to all those good times
I guess we had a ball
From Merthyr down to Hopkinstown
We must have played 'em all!

Recalling my days in the band
Carl Roberts (Bass Player)

A Man and Boy In Wales *By Carl Roberts*

49

Sleeping

Sleeping, sleeping
Nothing's quite like sleeping
Bodies switching off for the night
Batteries recharging
Fussing, rushing, barging
Lay undiscovered 'till the morning light

Sleeping, sleeping
Nothing's quite like sleeping
While physically abandoning our schemes
Bereft and unaware
We slumber without care
Oblivious to all except our dreams

Sleeping, sleeping
Nothing's quite like sleeping
Refreshment of the horizontal kind
Removed from those awake
And numb to parts that ache
We float away and leave the world behind